Love Letters with your Soul

Writing Your Way to Unconditional Love and Healing Wisdom

HEATHER C. WILLIAMS

For permission requests, write to the author at:
heathercwilliams@gmail.com

Author Name: Heather C. Williams

Publisher Name: Promoting Positivity Publishing
Contact Information: www.promotingpositivity.com

Love Letters with Your Soul
Heather C. Williams - 1st ed.

ISBN: 979-8-9871982-0-9

This book is dedicated to Dan, Hunter and Ireland.

You continually amaze me with your brilliance.

Thank you for your love.

It means everything to me.

CONTENTS

CHAPTER ONE

My Love Letter Journey

I started writing love letters the year that I turned 40. Not romantic love letters for someone else, but love letters to myself, my body and all aspects of my life. It was my attempt to heal and find inner peace. To try and make amends and make friends with everything.

I had been on a spiritual journey up until that point, but it didn't include all of me. It was more about positive affirmations and manifesting my best life possible. I could accept the good parts of myself, but the shameful, painful, fearful parts were not welcome at my party.

I became an expert at positively affirming the good and ignoring and casting out the bad. There was a lot of doing and trying to make things happen and willing it to be so. I would hear the whispers of my pain but I would not listen.

Then I started reading *A Course in Miracles* and everything began to change. This spiritual practice was less about learning and doing and more about unlearning, releasing, surrendering and being willing to see everything differently. It involved God and Christ consciousness, prayer and trusting in a higher power.

This was not something I had ever learned to do. I could never relate to a particular religion and I didn't like the idea of a judgmental God in the sky. But *A Course in Miracles* introduced me to a Divinely loving presence that is always here to guide us and to love us unconditionally. A wholeness and a holiness that exists within us all.

The daily lessons in *A Course in Miracles* opened my heart and mind. Their simplicity and power ran deep into my core, breaking up the old stories and ideas I had about myself, my life and the people in my life.

Some days I had "aha" moments that felt uplifting and enlightening, but most days I felt "oh no" moments. *Oh no, I didn't realize I was so judgmental with myself and others.*

In the midst of my ego breaking down, my body began to break down as well. I had digestion issues and adrenal fatigue. I was exhausted and in pain. It was as if my body said, *I can't live like this anymore Heather. I can't hold it all for you. I have tried to carry it all, but I can't do it anymore.*

I tried to fix my body with western medicine, eastern medicine, supplements, antibiotics, thyroid medication and elimination diets. When none of it healed me, I turned to energy medicine.

I started reading books on how to heal myself with Divine love. It all seemed impossible but I was desperate, so I kept an open mind. The first book I read said that if I have any unforgiveness in my life, it will block the healing process in my body. Then it asked, *who do you need to forgive?*

I remember feeling confused at that question. I thought I was at peace with my past and my life and I didn't think there was anyone I needed to forgive. Then I heard a voice in my mind say, *you need to forgive your body. You are mad at your body.*

I paused for a moment and thought about this. Am I blocking my healing process because I am mad at my body? And then as if someone turned on the lights, I could see into spaces and places I had never seen before.

I was shown all the frustration and disappointment I had felt over the years. All the mean comments I had thought or uttered about myself. All the sadness, shame and pain I had buried. I was at war with myself and my body and I did not even realize it.

As a teenager, I thought it was conceited to love and appreciate the body I was given, so I either picked at it, put it down or ignored it. Then in my 30s when I was trying to get pregnant and it wasn't working, I felt betrayed, scared and angry. I thought my body was failing me.

I felt such relief when I eventually got pregnant, but I could see that I was still carrying anger and frustration from that period of my life and from so many other points in my life as well.

It surprised me because I thought of myself as a grateful and happy person. I believed in the power of positive affirmations and the Law of Attraction. I actively used mantras and daily affirmations to stay positive. I literally wrote a book about the power of gratitude and how to write guided affirmations because I know how helpful they are. And I still use them and believe wholeheartedly in the importance of positivity and daily gratitude.

However, what I didn't understand was that I had old, painful emotions buried in my body and I couldn't affirm them away. I had to face the stuff I didn't want to face. A deep inner journey was calling to me and the first place I had to begin was with my body.

Tears began to fall and all I could say was "Oh my God, I am so sorry." I did not need to forgive my body; I needed my body to forgive me.

I wanted to apologize and dialogue with my body, so I picked up my journal and I began writing my body a love letter. It went something like this:

Dearest body,

I am so sorry. Please forgive me. You have only ever tried to serve me and in return I have beaten you down over and over again.

No wonder you feel sick. No wonder you are so tired. You don't feel safe with me.

I haven't treated you well, but today is a new day. I see you with fresh eyes. You are incredible and you deserve my love.

I vow to love you wholeheartedly from this moment forward. I vow to honor your magnificence. I vow to cherish you and take care of you.

Thank you for all that you have done for me every second of my life. You have stood by me through it all. You are a loyal and loving friend.

How can I help you feel better? How can I help you heal? I am listening, tell me what you need.

I love you and I am so grateful to have you.

Love,
Me

Then I kept the pen moving and I allowed my body to write me back.

Dearest Heather,

Thank you for reaching out and thank you for apologizing. It means so much to be seen and valued by you. I forgive you for everything.

I know you weren't trying to be mean to me. It was an unconscious habit and I know you will be kinder moving forward. I love you and I am here to serve you.

I am healing. What I need from you is love, kind thoughts and rest. You are carrying too much mentally and emotionally. You are trying to control and fix everything. It's not your job to do that.

Try to come into the present moment more often. Breathe, slow down, relax. Focus on all the things that are going well, right here, right now. There is so much to be grateful for.

Believe in our power to heal and thrive. Stay open and curious. We are Divinely guided and loved and the right solutions will flow to us. We can trust in the goodness of life.

I am ready to find a new harmonious way of co-existing together. I know we will feel better soon.

I love you and I love being loved by you.

Love,
Your body

I felt there was more to say so I continued our correspondence.

Dearest body,

Thank you for forgiving me. I am so lucky to have you. You have always been there for me.

You are my sacred home and you only deserve my love and appreciation. I am ready to change.

I will slow down and trust in the goodness of life. I will stay open and curious. I will rest in gratitude and believe in our power to heal and thrive.

I honor your strength and beauty. I am committed to your brilliance and I am devoted to your light.

I will honor you from this day forward and I surrender all my love to you.

Love,
Heather

As I re-read the letters, I had chills. A vow of love and truth had been made and a bridge of love and forgiveness was extended back to myself and back to my body. It was a new day, a new relationship, and a new beginning. This was the moment I began to heal.

Over the next few months, I wrote more love letters and I showed up for my body in helpful and loving ways. I welcomed in Divine love and I was willing to see everything with fresh eyes. My love letters helped me see the truth, tell the truth and receive the truth. They inspired me to take a stand for love and for love only.

Once I started trusting in the power of love more than the power of my problems, I lifted into a higher vibration, one where I was able to receive Divine help. Synchronistic solutions showed up easily. I was being guided and loved from a higher realm. It was undeniable grace.

I discovered a new doctor who was very helpful on my healing journey. I found new foods and new ways of eating that felt good in my body. I came across supplements and solutions that worked and my energy came bounding back to life.

I was on a new path of wholeness and vibrant health. My heart was open, my mind was available and my body had permission to heal and thrive in a loving environment. My love letters were a catalyst for healing because they were a safe space to be open and honest. They shifted me from denial and despair into curiosity and compassion.

This experience inspired me to take a closer look at all of my relationships and I began writing love letters to everything and everyone. Each time I engage in this process, I always feel relieved and inspired at how simple it is to get to the root of what I want and need. It's an energy shifting, miracle-working, divinely-guided experience. The comfort that comes through in the exchange of writing the love letter and then being responded to, feels very profound. I feel seen, heard, understood, loved and guided, all within a few minutes.

As a student and a teacher of spirituality and love, I have investigated and invested in many ways to find clarity and guidance in my life. Everything I have tried has been fascinating and helpful, but it required me to look outside of myself for guidance. The clearest crystal ball I have found has been when I turn within. I'm writing this book to remind you that you have access to an inner guidance system that is available in every moment.

The inner wisdom that comes through the love letter writing process is from a pure source of love that provides an outflow of guidance and clarity. I felt compelled to share it because this technique is easy to learn, it doesn't require a lot of time, it's free, and you can do it anywhere. It compliments any other healing modality you may be using now and the results are profoundly helpful.

The most miraculous part of this process is to witness how this simple internal correspondence can heal and make positive shifts externally in your life, with very little effort. As we cultivate more love and acceptance within ourselves, we bring more love and acceptance into the world and it creates a positive ripple effect across every area of our lives.

When I share this process with friends, family and clients, some are excited to jump in and try it and others are more hesitant. They say things like "I'm not a good writer" or "I wouldn't know what to say" or "I don't think this will work for me."

However, when they do try it, they are pleasantly surprised at what transpires and they are always in awe of the powerful truths that get revealed through their writing.

So, as you begin this journey with yourself, please remember that there is no right or wrong way to do this. It does not have to be perfect or polished. It will not be graded or judged.

Throughout the chapters, I will take you through the letter writing process. Personally, I like learning from examples, so I provide examples in each chapter. My hope is that my letters will inspire you to find your own path, so you can experiment and experience a cathartic release and healing in your own life circumstances.

Thank you for reading this book. Thank you for being open to the process of cultivating more love and wholeness in your life. Thank you for contributing more peace to our planet. I hope this book brings healing love, helpful insights and joyful harmony into all aspects of your life.

CHAPTER TWO

Love Letters with My Soul

After my love letter correspondence with my body, I began to crave more peace and love in all areas of my life. *A Course in Miracles* was helping me to release old, unhelpful patterns to make room for new, more enjoyable ways of being. I was meditating daily and feeling more connected to God and Divine Love. I was taking responsibility for my thoughts, behaviors, actions and happiness. After years of "Soul searching" and looking for things outside of myself to make me happy, turning within started to feel more normal and nourishing.

However, my ego was still very present in my life. It was loud and negative and disappointed all the time. The contrast between my ego and the love that was rising up made me feel like I had two different minds. I started to be curious about the difference between my ego mind and my loving mind.

I began to refer to my loving mind as my Soul. She was strong, kind, wise, helpful and loving. She would graciously open her arms to me and say "Look at you...you are amazing. I love you so much. You never have to earn my love. You are enough exactly as you are and I am here to love, protect and support you. I will never leave you."

My ego mind on the other hand, would cross its arms and say "I can't believe it...you screwed up again. No one will love you like this. You are broken. You need to do more and be more. How are we ever going to get through this? We are stuck again."

My Soul would turn to me and say "We are not stuck. Nothing is wasted. We can use it all. Take a deep breath. You are safe, loved, valuable and worthy. I am here to help and we will figure it out together. There are so many positive solutions and outcomes. Just be open and trust my love for you."

The difference between my ego and my Soul felt palpable and shocking. It became obvious that my ego mind wanted to beat me down and my Soul mind wanted to lift me up. I had spent most of my life unconsciously listening to my ego and I was ready to stop. I was excited to strengthen my relationship with my loving Soul, so I began writing her love letters.

When I write to my Soul, I share my gratitude with her and I ask for help and guidance. Then I keep the pen moving and I let her write me back. I allow myself to be deeply seen and unconditionally loved.

At first, I didn't know how to let that kind of love in, so I just imagined how much I loved my kids and then multiplied that love times infinity and gave it back to myself. I tried to see myself through the eyes of my wise, eternal, unconditionally loving Soul. The act of allowing myself to be seen and loved like that felt healing on so many levels.

I invite you to reach out to your Soul and to experience this loving interaction for yourself. It may feel awkward at first, but I promise that it gets easier with practice. I know that if this powerful guidance and unconditional love is available to me, then it is available to everyone.

Unconditional love has many names, so use the word that speaks to you. In this chapter, I use the word Soul, but I often write to God, Jesus, the Universe, or Divine love. If the word Soul isn't working for you and you prefer a different word to represent unconditional love, then please use it.

Don't let semantics stand in your way of connecting with this higher realm of wisdom and love. For the purposes of this chapter, I am saying Soul, but feel free to use the word that calls to you.

Here are some clues to help you find this unconditionally loving, Soulful part of yourself.

- Your Soul is patient, kind and loving.
- Your Soul is cheering you on always.
- Your Soul loves you no matter what.

Your Soul is a multi-faceted, wise, energetic entity. It has access to your past, present and future selves. Through your Soul, you can tap into your spirit, your higher self and Divine intelligence. Your Soul is connected to your body, relationships, emotions and potential.

Your Soul will love you beyond successes and failures, ups and downs, good days and bad days. The truth is that your Soul doesn't even recognize successes and failures. It doesn't categorize your life in the same way that your ego mind does. It doesn't compartmentalize or keep score. Your Soul just celebrates you, your aliveness, your presence, your spirit.

When we listen to our Soul, we begin to operate from a place of abundance and possibility and we can't help but make magical things happen. Opportunities come knocking, doors open to places beyond our wildest dreams and most importantly, we enjoy the journey along the way.

Do not underestimate the power of your Soul and your own inner wisdom. Writing your Soul a love letter is completely free and takes very little of your time, but the benefits are exponential. You will discover portals beyond space and time and tap into a loving life force that will always lead you into more clarity, peace and love.

Try it and be open to the kind, loving and wise advice you can receive in this interaction. Here is an example of one of my many love letters to my Soul.

My Dearest Soul,

Thank you for your limitless love. I am so relieved to receive your unconditional patience, kindness and acceptance. It feels like a healing balm on my heart.

At first your love felt foreign to me. I didn't know how to let it in. But I am ready now to hear you and to know you. Thank you for loving me no matter what.

I need and want your guidance and support in my daily life. I want to be better and to do better. I want to be loving, kind, carefree, relaxed and joyful.

I am so grateful for everything that I have, yet I still lose perspective a lot of the time. I want to channel your kindness, wisdom and love. I want to be so much more than I feel that I am. I want my actions to live up to my loving intentions.

How do I let go and trust more? How can I be more loving with myself and others? How do I hold it all better?

Thank you for helping me to forgive everything and everyone, including myself. Thank you for helping me to be open to receive all of the goodness and abundance in my life. Thank you for helping me to see the love and blessings that surround me everywhere.

I want to live a life full of purpose and love and make a positive difference in the world. Thank you for helping me do that.

I appreciate and admire you.

All my love,
Heather

Now I let my Soul write me back.

Dearest Heather,

Thank you for your sacred love letter. I am grateful that you hear me and I love that you want to know me. I am endlessly proud of who you are and I am so excited about all the beautiful possibilities in your life.

You are on a sacred life path. Keep focusing on love. Love is the only thing that matters.

Allow joy and abundance to pour into your experience. It's okay to trust in the goodness of yourself and your life. You can trust yourself. You can trust in the timing of it all. You can trust in love.

Relax and slow down. You don't have to make it all happen or figure it all out. You don't have to push to get it all done or do everything yourself. Allow yourself to be carried by the loving force of life.

Open your heart and surrender to the truth of love. Visualize peace and love reaching every cell of your being. Try to see yourself through my eyes. You are deeply loved and cared for and worthy of love.

And if you forget and you find yourself weighed down by life, let the heaviness be a gentle reminder. It feels heavy, overwhelming and too much to bear because you are trying to hold on to something that is not yours to carry.

Life loves you and supports you. Believe in the goodness of yourself and others. You are complete, whole and brilliant now.

Have fun and enjoy the day-to-day moments of your life. Enjoy it all and embrace it all and everything will thrive and open up from your loving light and your connection to all the goodness that surrounds you.

I am here for you and we are eternally connected. I will never leave you. I will always love you and together we will walk through this life with Divine love, ease and grace.

Here's to you living a life full of vibrant health, magical blessings, loving relationships, abundant success, joyful laughter and an endless flow of love!

I believe in your brilliance and I am always sending you love and light.

I love you here, now and always.

Love,
Your Soul

As I re-read my letter, I let my Soul's perspective and wisdom soak in. It felt like a permission slip to enjoy my life right here and now. The unconditional love, kindness and wisdom that came through, was unlike anything I had ever experienced. This level of love continues to bring waves of relief to my heart, mind and body.

We live in a world where most of the love we experience is conditional, so I know this exercise may feel abstract and challenging. It may feel weird to write kind and loving things about yourself. But I encourage you to try it anyway. The act of writing, with the intention to find an unconditionally loving side of yourself, will create a positive shift in your consciousness.

Your letter can be much less formal than my letter and more of an open dialogue or a stream of consciousness writing experience. Maybe you begin by writing down your thoughts about it all and just see what comes out. Again, there is no right or wrong way to do it.

The most important thing to remember is that this process is an opportunity to express your thoughts and emotions. It is a chance to tell the truth. It is a chance to be heard and loved.

I encourage you to be willing to see yourself through the eyes of your loving Soul. Be willing to let go of everything you thought you knew about who you are and what you are capable of being. Be willing to surrender to the truth of all that you are and all that you are becoming.

Follow the kind, loving voice of your Soul and you will always be guided back to love, to light and to your best life ever. When you nurture your Soul, your Soul will nurture you right back.

CHAPTER THREE

Love Letters to Help Your Body Thrive

As I shared in chapter one, expressing love to our bodies is a profoundly uplifting, healing and helpful act of love. Our body is a living, breathing, intelligent entity that has been with us since before our birth. It has a direct link to our every thought and experience and it is always growing, changing, adapting and learning.

Our body tells the story of our life. It holds it all. It is a loyal and loving friend that is here to serve us.

Now ask yourself, are you kind and loving to your body? Do your eyes light up when you see it looking back at you in the mirror? Do you treat it well? Do you think loving, kind thoughts about your body? If your body was another person, would it feel loved and appreciated by you?

Most of us answer 'no' to the above questions. We are somehow programmed to see the flaws and to under-appreciate the magnificence of what our bodies do for us every minute and every second of the day. Our bodies are loyal loving friends that show up for us, even if we consistently treat them poorly. And yet, bodies have breaking points and we need to find ways to love and nourish them so they can thrive.

Here is what I have learned and continue to learn. We need to be kind to our bodies now, in this moment, even if they are not "perfect". We must accept them, love them and appreciate them. Especially if we want to heal from an illness or an injury. Especially if we want to age gracefully. Especially if we want to experience vibrant health and spectacular energy.

If you already have a great relationship with your body and you don't have anything you need to heal, then I recommend writing your body a love letter filled with gratitude. Shower it in the love and appreciation it deserves. Be specific and celebrate the little things, the big things and everything in between.

Once you have pledged your love and appreciation, let your body write you back. Just be open to whatever comes out. This is a fast and effortless way to reconnect with this sacred part of you that has been with you every second here on planet earth.

As I mentioned in chapter one, writing my body love letters helped me immensely on my healing journey. Since then, I feel so much better in my body. However, bodies are always changing and evolving, so this is a process that I have done and will continue to do, over and over.

If I get sick or I am experiencing physical pain, I take a moment to dialogue with my body. I am always surprised at how much emotional pain and resistance comes up with the physical pain or illness. This is not a random coincidence. Our physical pain is directly linked to our emotional pain and when we acknowledge and address all aspects of ourselves, then we can get to the root cause, recover quicker and rediscover our health and wholeness.

Pain carries a powerful message and although our instinct is to numb it or to try and shut it down, I have found that it is helpful to bring attention to the pain in the present moment from a place of 'I see you, I feel you and I'm so sorry you are hurting, how can I help? What do you need from me?'

Below is an example of a love letter I wrote when I was experiencing pain in my left leg. The pain was piercing and strong and although I was getting help from a doctor, I wanted to connect with my leg energetically to clear the space, help speed up the healing process and assist in any way that I could.

Here was the correspondence that transpired.

Dearest body,

I am so sorry we are hurting. This pain is so strong. It takes my breath away and I hate the way I feel right now.

I normally feel really good and healthy and I can see how much I take you for granted on a regular basis. I am sorry for that. This pain is bringing up fear and sadness. It feels unbearable.

Please let me know how I can help you heal? How can I be kinder to you? How can I take better care of you? What do you need from me? What is at the root of this pain?

I want us to heal and feel incredible. I want to let go of any old patterns that aren't serving us, so that we can thrive and enjoy our life.

Thank you for everything you have given me.

I am open to receive your wisdom and I love and cherish you.

Love,
Heather

Dearest Heather,

Thank you, my love, for your heartfelt letter. I am so sorry this pain is so intense. I promise that we are healing, and you will feel better soon. I'm glad you found a great doctor to help us heal. We need outside help and support for this.

Thank you for your curiosity and openness to explore the deeper meaning of your pain. This pain is old energy leaving your body. It is an invitation to release the past and make way for a new way of being.

You currently carry too much. The distractions, the fear, the worry, the anxiety – they don't serve you mentally and the stress that comes from the fear and worry does not serve our body.

We must have daily practices that release our stress. We must slow down and make space for peace and love to flow. We must hold a vision for vibrant health, wholeness and healing.

Life loves and supports you, but life needs you to stay awake, grateful and present. When you aren't present, you miss the gifts and miracles that are trying to come to you. The channel needs to remain open in order to receive.

So, relax and let go of all the stuff that keeps you separate and out of the flow of your life. Let go of the stress, worry, self-doubt, painful memories, judgments, ideas of how it "should be." Be willing to see yourself in a new way.

Use your energy towards positive momentum so you can find solutions. Visualize what you want, live in gratitude, find peace in your mind, take positive action and live from your loving heart.

This takes a fierce commitment to love. You have the capability to do this. Your devotion and commitment to love will help us both heal on the deepest level possible.

I love you and I believe in your strength and capacity to love and thrive.

I am healing and serving you always.

Love,
Your body

This simple and profound correspondence with my body brought me relief, comfort, guidance, wisdom and peace of mind. It gave me a space to express my pain and ask for help and it gave my body a voice and a chance to be heard. A few days later, the pain in my leg was gone and I felt relieved, grateful and whole again.

The act of facing our pain is healing on so many levels. Our physical and psychological pain carries emotional energy and it wants to be acknowledged. My instinct has often been to try to numb or push through it. However, when I turn toward the pain, and be with it and listen to what it needs, it transforms.

Try corresponding with your body when you have pain, illness or discomfort. Be curious and open about what message the pain may be carrying for you. Be willing to see it all with a different perspective.

If you need to have surgery or any medical procedure, take a moment and slow down. Close your eyes, place your hand on your heart and take a few deep breaths. Send love to every cell in your body. Visualize your body receiving a miraculous healing.

In addition to blessing your own body, send blessings of love, gratitude and healing light to the doctors, nurses, staff, other patients and the facility or hospital where you will be going. Imagine the doctors and nurses having the best day of their lives. They are Divinely guided, divinely focused and in the flow of excellence.

Have a conversation with your body about the procedure you are going to have. You can do this in your mind, out loud or on paper. Explain what is going to happen, why you are doing this and how it is going to make things better. Set an intention that you are ready to receive a healing and you are open to finding healing solutions.

The act of sending love and taking a few moments to dialogue with your body, makes space for a successful surgery and recovery. Coming into communion with your body and the people involved with helping your body heal, will help the process run more smoothly.

I also encourage you to spend a few minutes every day imagining yourself experiencing vibrant health. If you haven't ever felt that, then make it up and write it out. How do you look, how do you feel, what is your life like with a vibrant, healthy, energetic body?

I have included a guided affirmation that I created to cultivate vibrant health in my body. I wrote it from a best case scenario point of view and it helps me claim my birth right of health and wholeness.

Even if I am not feeling great in my body, this affirmation holds a vision for what is possible and for how I deeply desire to feel in this moment. There is great power when we take a stand for our health and wellness.

Vibrant Health and Wellness Affirmation:

I trust in my body and its ability to heal and recover. I trust in my Divine DNA and my birthright of health and wholeness. I open my arms to experiencing vibrant health and wellness right here, right now.

My body is healthy and strong. My immune system is resilient and powerful. My mind is peaceful and I radiate brilliant, intelligent loving energy everywhere I go.

I am exceptional at taking care of my body, mind, and spirit, and I thrive in my life. I feel light, carefree, youthful, zenful, wise and happy.

I am in the best shape of my life and I am so grateful for my body. I stay connected to my breath and I take deep, cleansing breaths all day long.

When it is time for bed, I fall asleep naturally and easily and I sleep peacefully throughout the night. In the morning I wake up rested, energized and excited to start a new day.

I put healthy, delicious, nourishing food in my body. I stay hydrated and I make time to stretch and move my body. My hormones, mood, and energy levels are in balance, and it feels great to be me.

I recommit and reconnect to my highest vision and purpose for myself every day. I take big leaps and baby step towards accomplishing my goals, my dreams, and my aspirations.

I am kind and gentle with myself like a true loving friend, and I love and accept myself completely. I love what I see when I look in the mirror and I feel amazing inside and out.

I am exceptional at feeling joyful and happy, soaking in the present moment, and showering the people I love with love. I am able to accomplish anything I set my mind to with ease and enjoyment.

I love and cherish my body and I am grateful for everything it has given me and continues to give me on a daily basis.

Every breath gives me an opportunity to make a positive difference, to have more fun, and to spread love and light into everything I do. My life is meaningful, full of heart and worth living.

Thank you body. Thank you for being healthy and strong. Thank you for standing with me through it all. Thank you for letting me experience and live my beautiful life.

Allow these affirmations to wash over you and sink in. Use the love letters to reunite and reconnect with your body. Give it your undivided attention for a few moments every day.

Listen deeply, ask empowering questions, invite whole, vibrant health into your day-to-day moments. I know you will be pleasantly surprised at how quickly your body will respond to your love and appreciation.

CHAPTER FOUR

Love Letters with Time

I know a lot of people, myself included, who feel like they don't have enough time. In fact, I am pretty sure that "I don't have enough time" is an unconscious mantra that we tell ourselves every day.

We accidentally affirm that we don't have enough time to do the things we love, not enough time to hang out with our family and friends, not enough time to finish projects, not enough time to sleep and care for ourselves and not enough time to follow our dreams.

Time is a small, simple word and yet it is packed with big emotions, perceptions and concepts. It seems to linger constantly in the backdrop of life. We can't help but think about it in all its facets.

'What time is it?' 'What time do I have to be there?' 'How much time do I have?' 'Time flies.' 'Time is going by so slowly.' 'I wish I had more time.' 'I never have enough time.'

I am definitely having a relationship with time. But it wasn't until I stepped back and examined my relationship with time that I realized, it was not a healthy relationship and I should try to improve it.

Time is an interesting phenomenon. It flies when we are having fun and it drags when we are stuck in traffic. Our experience with it isn't consistent, so is it possible that we never feel like we have enough time because we are constantly telling ourselves that we don't have enough time? Perhaps it is just something we have been conditioned to believe and, therefore, we simply need a program upgrade.

For this love letter writing exercise, have an open and honest conversation with time. Explore how you currently interact with it and be curious about how you would like to feel with time.

Visualize and imagine what it would feel like to have an abundance of time. What would you do with yourself if you had more time? What do you love to do in life?

Here is an example of what I wrote, and it quickly changed my relationship with time for the better.

Dearest Time,

I want to be friends with you. I can see that I have been trying to control you for as long as I can remember. I think about you all the time and I always wish I had more of you. Or if I'm bored, I may want less of you. Either way, it has been a very confusing relationship.

There is so much I want to do and get done and despite all of my efforts of trying to manage you, I still waste you and somehow never have enough of you.

I don't want to feel rushed and squeezed by you anymore. I feel victimized by my perceived lack of time and the length of my to-do list. Overwhelm is often my normal resting state and I won't waste my life in this way anymore.

So Time, please hear me. I need a program upgrade. I need a new and improved relationship with you. I am ready to step into new territory and higher, more joyful realms of being with you.

I want to have more fun and enjoy my day-to-day moments. I want to exist in real time, keeping my mind from drifting into the past and the future. I want to live in the present, doing things that I love with the people I love.

I am surrendering all of my previous concepts of time and I am open to receiving an abundance of joyful and peaceful time in my life.

Thank you, Time, for every timeless and magical moment you have given me!

I am eternally grateful for you.

Love,
Heather

And now I let Time write me back, so I know that my letter and message was received.

Dearest Heather,

Thank you for your letter and for your love. I hear you and I am ready to help you have a better experience with time.

I am glad you want to spend your time on earth doing things that you love and being with the people you love. That is what your time should be used for. It is amazing what you can accomplish and be when you live life from a place of love.

Time is on your side and time is here for you so you can live your best life. Let yourself enjoy the time you have been given. Feel grateful and slip into the present moment as much as possible. As you know, it is the only moment of time that is real.

You are the timeless author of your own story and there is nothing standing in your way of creating and living a life you love.

I love you and I am here for you to enjoy, laugh, live, give and love.

Eternally and lovingly yours,
Time

I love this process because whenever I do it, my relationship with time shifts. I move from feeling victimized to empowered and as a result, pockets of time open up for me that didn't exist before. It is immediate, and it is extremely helpful.

When we examine our experience with time and we get clear on what we want and how we want to feel, we open a door to a new way of being. And once we start to feel into what is possible, then we will create a new reality. A new reality that we love.

Let's begin a love affair with time and imagine that we have enough time to live a life doing the things that we love doing. Take a stand and commit to a new way of existing. Like a computer receiving an upgrade, reprogramming our relationship with time is not any different.

We have 1,440 minutes every day, so let's devote some of our time to improving our relationships so we can enjoy our precious time spent here on earth doing the things we love most.

CHAPTER FIVE

Love Letters with Money

Money is a powerful currency in our lives. We need it to survive and we need it to thrive. For some, money flows naturally and easily. For others it is a struggle to get it and to keep it.

As I began to explore my relationship with money, I could see how entangled I was with it. Family values, societal beliefs, collective fears and my own experiences with it were wrapped around me like a straitjacket.

Similar to my experience with time, I could see how my relationship with money needed a reboot. I appreciated the money I had, but somehow it never felt like enough and I was always fearful of losing it.

The thought of repairing, healing and upgrading my relationship with money sounded helpful and important, so I began by writing an honest and open love letter to it.

Here is the correspondence that unfolded.

Dearest Money,

I don't know where to begin. I am discovering how multi-layered my relationship is with you and it is very enlightening and alarming all at the same time.

I love having you in my life and I am so grateful for your presence and existence and yet you never feel like enough. I am so terrified of losing you or not having enough of you that I don't even let myself enjoy what I do have.

My relationship with you feels limited, restricted, and strained and I would love to find a new, harmonious way of existing and collaborating with you. I am so sorry for all the restrictions I have put on you. I'm sorry for all the pain and suffering that I have involved you in. It has been dysfunctional and unhealthy.

I have often treated you like you are never enough. That is unfair and untrue. You have been good to me and I am so grateful for your presence in my life.

I want to have a renewed, joyful, abundant relationship with you. I want to stop hoarding you, fearing your absence, fearing losing you, worrying about you, thinking it would all feel better, safer, more fun and more carefree if I just had more of you. But what does that even mean?

I have put so much pressure on you to provide my safety, my freedom, my comfort and my happiness. I have burdened you with my fears and worries of lack. I have craved you, cursed you and made you my savior. Please forgive me for my judgments and for the irrational power I have given you.

You are money. You are green and helpful and fun and important. You are necessary and valuable. You make me feel safe when I have more than enough and unsafe when I feel like I don't have enough.

I love it when you flow to me. I love knowing that I have more than enough of you. I love the idea of you overflowing abundantly into my life. I want to cherish and appreciate you, but I don't want to depend on you for my safety, security, sanity or happiness.

Thank you for showing me how to love you, collaborate with you and enjoy you. Thank you for helping me cherish you and share you. You bring important and helpful gifts into the world and I am ready to have a generous, joyful, empowering and grateful relationship with you.

I love you. I appreciate you. I'm grateful for all the wonderful things you have allowed me to enjoy; healthy food, a beautiful home, cars, vacations, adventures, school, gifts, fun. You have showered me with loving luxuries and I am ready to receive your gifts with grateful grace and love and to cherish you in healthy, happy, abundant ways.

Thank you to every person who has given me money or supported me financially. Thank you to every job or opportunity that has allowed me to make money. Thank you to my future abundance and prosperity that is joyfully headed my way.

I am ready to have a harmonious relationship with you. I am open to new possibilities. I am deeply grateful for all that you have given me!

I love, respect and appreciate you.

Love,
Heather

Dearest Heather,

Thank you for your letter and for your honest reflection of our relationship. I feel a burden has been lifted and I appreciate your gratitude and kind words. I recognize your readiness and willingness to move into a harmonious and loving relationship with me. I am ready for that too.

I am here to serve and be of service. Let's join together and enjoy the rich beauty that life has to offer. We exist in an abundant, bountiful, loving Universe and there is more than enough for everyone.

Put your faith in the miraculous and infinite power and potential of our abundant Universe and you will always live in the overflow. Marinate and meditate in the energy of all is well and all needs are met. Allow your cup to be generously filled with vibrant health, wealth and prosperity.

Spend time every day acknowledging the richness of life. Celebrate your own successes as well as the prosperity and successes of others. It is all evidence that abundance exists everywhere, always and in all ways. Celebrate the truth of that.

I welcome our new beginning and I am excited to flow freely into your life. Thank you for being willing to release the shackles, the fear and the dysfunction. It is causing unnecessary worries and stress in your life.

Relax knowing that I am here for you and I will always be here for you. I am your friend. I am on your side and I am here to help you grow and thrive.

I love you and I am here with you now and always.

Love your friend and ally,
Money

When I re-read what money had written to me, I was struck by the thought of money being an ally in my life. Before this correspondence, my relationship with money felt like it was over there and I was over here, with a wall in between us. But now, I could feel us standing together, side by side, united as friends. A loving bond had been formed and a new love began to flow.

My relationship with money is one that I continue to revisit. Old habits and patterns resurface and I have written multiple love letters to money over the years.

I am happy to report that I have a much more harmonious and loving relationship with money and as a result money flows into my life more abundantly and easily.

I am no longer blocking the flow of money with a scarcity mindset. I marinate and meditate in the energy of all is well and all needs are met. I am grateful for what I have and I am open to prosperity showing up in miraculous ways with ease and grace.

Try this exercise out. Explore your relationship with money. Be open and honest with yourself. If money was a person, what is the quality of your relationship?

Are you friends? Do you trust each other? Are you grateful for what you have? Are you frustrated or angry about what you don't have? What do you want to say to money? What would you want money to say to you?

If money has always been available to you, then take a moment to thank it for being in your life. If money has been a struggle, then spend some time making friends with it again. Set an intention for a new experience with money that feels prosperous, healthy and joyful.

After you correspond with money, you can create an affirmation to say daily. One of mine is:

Thank you Love and Money for flowing to me with Divine ease and grace and for exponentially growing, thriving and multiplying every day in uplifting, joyful and helpful ways.

I open my arms to you with gratitude and love.

It is important to feel grateful for what we have and celebrate what is coming. What we appreciate appreciates, and the energy of money will flow more abundantly into our lives if we welcome it home with open arms.

CHAPTER SIX

Love Letters with Your Loved Ones

I want to be a guiding force for love in my family and in the world. I try to be kind and loving to myself and others. And although I have the best intentions, sometimes the daily responsibilities of life, my unconscious behaviors and my worries and fears get in the way. To get back on track, I write love letters to my loved ones and then let them write back to me.

Let me be clear. The other person is not actually writing me back. I am still the one with the pen to paper, but I allow that person's voice to come through and speak to me from their perspective. I know it may sound a little strange, but the healings that I have received from these interactions are liberating and profoundly transformative.

It's like tapping into a magical, energetic realm in our Universe that goes beyond what we can see, hear and touch. After I dialogue in this way, things always shift for the better. Forgiveness takes place, healings occur, people are set free and love moves into the driver's seat.

This exercise is about expanding our awareness and perspective. It is a powerful, quick and surprisingly easy journal exercise and yet it creates exponential positive effects. Quite frankly, it's pure and amazing magic.

You can do this with anyone in your life, but it's especially helpful with the people you love the most and spend the most time with. We all feel each other's energy either consciously or unconsciously. There is an unspoken vibration flowing within and all around us and if we are out of alignment with love, then relationships can feel strained, confusing or off track.

The love letter writing process allows us to clear the air without having to have a lengthy talk about it. If after the letter writing correspondence you feel like something needs to be addressed or shared in real life, then you will be able to communicate your feelings with more clarity, composure and compassion.

One place in life that I especially want to soar with love, is in my relationships with my children. And yet sometimes, I feel like my love gets lost in translation through the daily responsibilities of parenting and our interactions. One way I recalibrate and return to a loving space is to write them a love letter and to let them write back. As I tune into their spirit and their deepest needs, I am able to write from their perspective.

I don't overthink it. It's not a mental exercise. It's a heart to heart connection. Once you try it yourself, you will understand. The pen will move and the right words that need to be said will come through.

I am always humbled at the wisdom, love and clarity that flows in. It helps me tap back into gratitude and the deeper truth about what my role needs to be as a mom. It helps me dissolve worries and gain wisdom. It helps me to forgive myself and let go. It helps me focus on what really matters and shift from fear to love.

I have written countless love letters to my kids throughout the years, but the example I am including is a love letter I wrote to my son Hunter when he was ten-years-old. He was changing so much at that point. Becoming more independent, needing me less. A part of me felt like I was losing him and our connection felt strained. I sat down before I went to bed that night and I wrote to him to clear the energy, tap back into the love and feel into the sacred depths of our relationship.

Dearest Hunter,

Let me start by saying I love you so much. I know I say those words a lot, so let me tell you why I love you.

You are loving, thoughtful, smart, kind, curious, open-hearted and fun to be around. You have always inspired me with your gentle spirit, your passion for life, and your persistence with solving puzzles and trying new things. You don't give up easily and you want to participate in life. I really admire that about you.

From the moment I held you in my arms, I knew I was lucky to be your mom. I felt waves of love wash over me unlike anything I had ever experienced. I also felt great responsibility to protect you and keep you safe. It was overwhelming at times to hold it all.

I have only ever wanted to love you. But I know there have been times where my fears and worries guided me in the wrong direction and I am sorry for any unnecessary pain I have caused you. I pray that you are set free from any mistakes I made along the way.

Thank you for loving me so deeply. Thank you for being gentle and kind with me. The first baby is often a bit of a guinea pig but you have always been patient and loving with me.

You are growing up right before my eyes. It is incredible to witness. It makes me happy and sad all at the same time. I need to keep up with your independence and your desire to do more on your own.

I need your help. Something feels off between us and I feel like I am losing you and that breaks my heart. Please tell me what you need from me.

How can I support you and love you better? I know I need to adapt and recalibrate. I welcome in Divine love, guidance and help in navigating all aspects of our relationship.

I want to be close with you through it all. I want to be a guiding source of love, acceptance and joyful support. I want us to laugh together and have fun. I want to feel connected to you through all your ages and stages of life.

Thank you for everything Hunter. You are one of my greatest teachers and you have taught me so much about love. I am so proud to call you my son.

I love you. I will always love you. And I will always love being loved by you.

Sending you blessings of love now and always.
Love,
Mommy

And now, I let him write back.

Dearest Mommy,

Thank you for writing to me. I love you so much. I know you do so much for me everyday and I don't always notice, but today I am saying thank you. I really do appreciate your time, your effort and your loving heart.

I know you care so deeply about me. I see you trying so hard to do everything right but I am not asking for you to be perfect. You can relax. Everything is good between us.

When I feel your pride, encouragement and your loving support, it's like oxygen for my Soul. But I also feel your fear, worry and stress and that is not helpful for either of us.

Please trust me. Trust that I will make good decisions. Trust that I am Divinely guided, just as you are. Give me space to be me.

Our relationship is changing but you are not losing me. I want to be close and connected to you always. I love being loved by you and I love loving you.

I am so grateful that you are my mommy.

I love you with all of my heart!

Love,
Hunter

The act of writing to Hunter allowed me to see everything from a different perspective. It gave me permission to be open and honest and to apologize and ask for help. It provided me a space to vent and also to deeply listen and tune into his needs.

I was able to have a profound conversation with my ten-year-old son that may or may not have been possible in real life. My highest self was in communion with his highest self and after this correspondence, I felt more relaxed, more trusting and more available.

The next day provided us with a new and improved experience. Peaceful and loving harmony was flowing between us. We were laughing and having fun and any disconnect from the day before had miraculously melted away.

I have done this exercise so many times with just about everyone in my family and every single time I experience a profound and uplifting shift that is felt on many levels.

You can do this exercise with anyone you know. The first letter allows you to express your gratitude but it can also be an opportunity for you to explain your actions, express your concerns, release frustration, apologize if you need to and ask for help and guidance.

The second letter is a chance for that person to hear you, love you, forgive you, praise you and guide you back to love.

This simple love recalibration is undeniably helpful, so I hope you try it out in your own life and in your own relationships.

One huge benefit that I have discovered from this writing exercise is that it gets me back in touch with all the specific things I love about the people I love. I see them with fresh eyes. I find it easy to compliment them and share my love, pride and admiration with them.

I don't need to tell them that I wrote a letter to help our relationship. I can simply say, "I was thinking about you today and I am so grateful that you are in my life. It is an honor to know you, to love you and to be loved by you. Thank you for everything."

Love is healing. Love is contagious in the best way. Love is absolutely free and yet it is one of the most valuable gifts we can give to each other.

Saying "I love you" is important, but when we tell someone why we love them, it is transformative. Don't underestimate the importance of sharing your love. It will bring more harmony and peace into all of your relationships.

CHAPTER SEVEN

Love Letters with Your Younger Self

If you have ever been fascinated with time travel, then you will love this exercise. Reconnecting with your younger self is profoundly transformative. It allows you to examine your life and your life circumstances from a unique perspective. You have a chance to comfort, encourage, apologize and explain yourself. You have an opportunity to forgive, let go and heal. I have revisited many different ages and stages in my past and I feel lighter and happier afterward, as if I have released and set free a trapped part of myself.

Allow yourself to think back to a time in your life when you needed clarity, comfort and guidance. Imagine you could go back in time and say anything to this part of yourself. What would you say? What would you have wanted to hear at that time in your life? What loving words can you express that will create a healing in your life?

Throughout my life, there are parts of me and memories that I enjoy thinking about. Stories that I love to tell, experiences that are fun to relive. And then there are parts of me that I don't want to remember or think about. Experiences that make me feel sad or ashamed. Times in my life that I wish had been different or that hadn't happened at all. Once I felt comfortable with the letter writing process, I made it a point to revisit myself along my journey.

I have done this time travel exercise many times with the intention to reconnect and reclaim myself, but the letter I want to share was when I reconnected with my 19-year-old self. It was 1994, my sophomore year in college. I was holding it together on the outside, but on the inside I felt like I was imploding.

My boyfriend and I had just broken up, my aunt who I was very close with was diagnosed with a brain tumor and I started to feel anxious all the time. Nowadays, it's very common to openly talk about anxiety and panic attacks, but at the time I didn't know what was happening to me or what to do about it. The Internet was not the resource it is today, so I was not able to diagnose myself with Dr. Google.

I was scared to tell anyone because I was afraid I was going crazy. Rather than getting help from a professional, I hid my panic and anxiety from everyone I knew and loved. I was ashamed of myself and I felt like damaged goods. I felt unlovable and alone. I eventually got help and found ways to cope with the anxiety, but I have never wanted to revisit that period in my life.

However, in an effort to love, heal and reclaim all aspects of myself, I knew I had to try to correspond with this part of myself. I grabbed my journal and a pen, and this is what quickly transpired.

Dearest 19-year-old self,

I just realized that I abandoned you. I turned away from you when you needed me most and I am so sorry. I'm here for you now.

You can trust me. You are not alone anymore. I love you and I accept you and I am here to help you heal and to set you free.

Tell me everything you need to say. I can handle it now. I am listening, and I love you.

Love,
Heather (at age 41)

Dearest Heather (at age 41),

Thank you so much for coming back for me. I have felt alone and scared and to have you here with me now feels comforting. I am so lost.

I need help, but I am terrified to ask for help. I am terrified to show people that I am vulnerable. I am scared to tell the truth.

I feel so unlovable and crazy right now. I am flooded with fear and anxiety and I feel like damaged goods.

What if no one will ever love me again? What if I feel anxious forever? What if I never feel safe again? What if I really am crazy?

I know I need help, but I'm not sure where to turn. Please help me. Please help me to know what to do.

Love,
Heather (at age 19)

Dearest Heather (at age 19),

Thank you for opening up to me.

I hear you and I can feel the pain and fear that you are feeling.

I am here for you and I can help you heal and feel lovable again.

You are safe. You can trust me. The fear and anxiety will pass soon. Everything is going to work out and all is well, even though it doesn't feel like it right now.

Let me share with you the exceptional path that life has in store for you. All this fear you feel, it's just fear you are feeling. You are not this fear. This fear does not define you.

Your courage is stronger than your fear. Your love is stronger than your fear. You are strong, worthy and lovable.

In the next few years you will finish college, studying a degree you love. You will love and be loved again. You will have joyful adventures and travel to beautiful parts of the world.

At age 25, you will meet a kind and loving man who will become your partner, your husband and the father of your two extraordinary children.

Your family and your children are more glorious than you could ever imagine. You are a deeply caring mom to your kids and a loving, compassionate person in life. I am so proud of who you are now and who you are continually becoming.

You have permission to trust and relax into the goodness of your life. You are set free. You don't have to figure everything out. You can relax into the miraculous flow of your life. Life loves you and supports you.

Forgive and let go of anyone and anything that has ever hurt you. Set everyone free with love so that you can set yourself free with love. Life has always been on everyone's side.

Laugh, relax, do things that make you feel happy and follow your heart. You have permission to fall in love with yourself and your life.

I love you and I will always love you.

Love,
Heather (at age 41)

Dearest Heather (at age 41),

Wow. Thank you so much. I feel like I can breathe again. I feel like I can love and accept myself again. Thank you so much for this lifeline.

Thank you for telling the truth and for helping me to heal. I am so relieved. I can relax. I feel loved and accepted.

Thank you for coming back for me. I'm ready to heal and forgive. I set everyone free and send them off with love.

Thank you. Thank you so much. I am so grateful to finally be free. I love you.

Love,
Heather (at age 19)

After I finished this correspondence, I sat back in amazement as tears streamed down my face. I felt like I had traveled back in time and was standing with her. It felt so real and at the end I had an image of my 19-year-old self smiling and laughing. She was so grateful that I came back for her. She was so grateful to be set free.

These techniques can lead to a powerful healing. It felt sacred to travel back to my younger self with my current wisdom and perspective. My current self knows that everything is going to be okay. I can see that the path my life took was perfect and how everything worked out in more extraordinary ways than I ever could have imagined. Even when I couldn't see it in the moment.

I encourage you to try this exercise with yourself. Revisit these parts from your past. What do you need to say? What do you need to hear? What do you need to heal, forgive and let go of?

I continue to use this healing exercise and I have traveled back in time over and over again. I have visited and revisited all ages and versions of myself. So many parts of me needed to be seen, heard, loved and accepted.

Abandoning myself during hard times was a pattern and going back and loving those parts of myself was and continues to be a significant part of my healing journey. It has been a fascinating experience that has taught me so much about life, true acceptance and the healing power of unconditional love.

I find this exercise particularly helpful with the younger childhood years. Between the ages of 0-10 years old, we do not have a lot of authority over our lives and we can find ourselves in uncomfortable, painful and shameful situations. Even if our childhood was great and our parents and caregivers did the best they could, many of us are left with accumulated pain and trauma from that time period in our lives.

When we go back to our child self and really listen to what he or she needs, which is usually some form of love, we heal that wounded part of ourselves. The wounds and traumas of our past, cause emotional and physical discomfort and dis-ease in our current lives. When we go back and heal a past wound, we feel better in the present moment.

When I connect with my child self through my writing or in my meditations, I sit with her. I let her cry. I let her express her anger. I allow her to say and feel things that she never could have said or felt at the time.

I hold her in my arms and I love her. I am able to be a source of strength and unconditional love for her in her most vulnerable and raw moments. I am the one she has been waiting for and together we help each other rise up and heal.

This level of healing has been a gift in my life and I hope it will be a gift in yours. Give yourself permission to go back and comfort, encourage and nurture these aspects of who you are.

Collect yourself and love yourself up. Let your younger self be heard and let your younger self be set free. It will enlighten your mind and lighten your spirit.

CHAPTER EIGHT

Love Letters with Your Older, Wiser Self

Now that you have time traveled to the past, it's time to travel to the future and reach out to your older, wiser self. This is a helpful way to shift your perspective and gain clarity around your current circumstances.

Create an image in your head of an older version of yourself. It could be 20 years from now, 50 years from now or 5 years from now. The most important thing to remember is that this person has already lived into your phenomenal future and they have so much wisdom and perspective to share with you.

This is a glimpse into your best life imaginable. It is like having access to your own crystal ball, so use this process to ease concerns about your future, gain clarity around a specific life decision, and receive support, love, encouragement and guidance.

You can be vulnerable with this part of yourself. What kind of things would you want to know from your future self? What kind of things would you want your future self to tell you? What do you need guidance or clarity around?

Here is an example of a correspondence with my older, wiser self. I usually reach out to her when I need a pep talk and she guides me out of fear and back into love. She has already lived my future and she knows that everything works out in wonderful ways.

Dearest older, wiser self,

I feel overwhelmed and worried right now and I need your help. I want to be amazing and yet I keep falling flat on my face. I'm tired, my kids are grumpy and the negative voices in my head keep chanting something about me being worthless.

I feel anxious, afraid and uncomfortable. I don't want to feel like this anymore. Am I doing something wrong? I'm embarrassed to even write this because I feel like I should have all of this figured out by now.

Can you please shed your wise and helpful perspective on my life right now? I need and want your help.

Thank you for your guidance, wisdom and love.

Love,
Heather

Dearest Heather,

Thank you for reaching out to me. I love you and I always love helping you. I am so proud of you and everything that you are. Try to remember to take a deep breath and relax. Life has never let you down, and it isn't going to start now.

You are safe. You are loved and cared for. You are not alone. Have faith in the goodness of life.

Let me break it down for you. This is a moment in time. A precious moment in time. Do not waste it in fear. Do not waste it in worry. Stop getting seduced by the worry and the fear. You are smarter and stronger than that.

Take a stand for your well-being and trust in the love and support that is all around you. Faith is not a feeling, faith is a choice. Your family is precious. Your kids are remarkable. Enjoy them now. Enjoy the sweetness that is all around.

Even the grumpy faces and whining voices are precious in their own way. Be the mom you know you are capable of being. Take a stand for love. You know that love is the only thing that matters, so take a stand for it and push everything else aside.

The self-doubt, the worry and the negative voices in your head - try to stop taking it all so seriously. Send the bully in your mind love and compassion. She is just scared, and you don't need to let her guide you anymore. You can take control of your happiness. Set yourself free. Laugh now. Be carefree now. Relax now.

You are brilliant and amazing so allow yourself to be brilliant and amazing. You are going to have so much fun in your life, if you let yourself. Love and abundance is flowing all around you, so let yourself enjoy it and trust in the magic of your magnificent life.

I have lived your future and it is undeniably miraculous. Trust, surrender, let go and forgive. You will be blown away by the wondrous gifts life will continue to bring you.

Open your arms. Open your heart. Open your mind. You have permission to enjoy it all now and forever and I insist you follow my advice and orders.

I love you and I will always love you no matter what.

Love,
Older, wiser Heather

When I finish any correspondence with my older and wiser self, I always feel relieved, comforted and re-inspired. She is loving, confident, and direct and she always helps me refocus on what is most important in my life. She gives me the loving wakeup call that I need.

Try this exercise in your own life when you need a pep talk or guidance. Let your older, wiser, self, support you, encourage you and guide you back to love.

CHAPTER NINE

Love Letters for Forgiveness

Now that we have traveled back in time and forward into the future, we are ready to go beyond space and time. Love letters for forgiveness can be a deeply transformative experience. In this exercise, you let your loved ones or anyone you need to forgive, living or deceased, write to you.

We all have people in our life that we feel have wronged us in some way. Maybe they didn't love us in the way we needed to be loved or maybe they were cruel or hurtful. Whatever the reason, holding onto unforgiving, resentful thoughts about anyone is only holding ourselves hostage.

We don't forgive to let the other person off the hook for what they did. We forgive to set ourselves free from the past pain that is keeping us stuck and hurting us in the present moment. I think most of us understand why we should forgive and most of us want to forgive, but often it's hard to let go of the pain.

I feel strongly about the power and necessity of this particular exercise. I think in order to truly forgive someone, it helps to understand why they did what they did. If we can see life from their perspective, maybe we can acquire the level of compassion it takes to forgive.

If I need to forgive someone, I ask myself, *what would it take for me to forgive them. What would they have to say in order to make it all better? Is there anything that they could say that would help me move on from this pain? What would it feel like to hear or read an apology from them? Would it help me feel less chained to this pain?* And then I put pen to paper and I write to myself as if I was that person apologizing to me and I allow myself to hear everything I need to hear in order to move on.

The example in this chapter is a letter between my mom's mother and herself. My mom had a challenging relationship with her mother. She never felt loved or accepted by her and it negatively affected many areas in her life.

One day my mom mentioned some sadness and pain around her relationship with her mother. Her mother had passed away seven years prior. I was surprised at how present the pain was, even though the person who caused the pain had passed years before.

That is when I suggested that my mom write herself a love letter from her mother, but write it as if her mother was writing it to her. I told her to let her mother shower her in pride and admiration. To let her explain herself and apologize. To let her love her in the way she always wished she could have been loved.

After my mom wrote the letter, she let me read it. My mom is a writer and I have read almost everything she has ever published, and this was not my mom's writing. I knew my mom's mother and I could feel her spirit throughout the letter. It was profound.

I had my mom write her mother back, this time as herself. It amazed me how her perspective had shifted and softened. She was able to accept her mother's apology. She was able to see and to hear her on a different level and most importantly, she was able to begin the process of forgiving and letting go.

Here is the correspondence that occurred, through this writing exercise, between my mom's mother and my mom Diane.

Dear Diane,

This is a hard letter to write because I will have to admit things that are hard for me to face, let alone tell you.

First of all, I see now how I harmed you and how much that hurt you and I'm sorry, so sorry for that. I am not going to justify it or say 'I did the best I could' because I can see that I could have done so much better.

I could have loved you so much better. You were sweet and good and innocent and strong, so strong willed. And so beautiful.

I was jealous of how you loved your dad and I see now that I could also have felt that love, your love, if I would have loved you, but I did not. So sad. I covered over my love with jealousy, anger and insecurity, so that there was no room for the love. So of course you loved your dad and avoided me.

Inside, I was aching, the unloved child and that is the pain that I caused you. Very sad and unforgivable. I am working to forgive myself as I know you are working to forgive me.

When I criticized your job choices it was because I knew how smart and able you are. I wanted you to be the powerful and brilliant person you could be, a lawyer, not selling books or healing people. When you struggled with money, it angered me that you, who were so able, should struggle.

But now I see that you were trying to heal yourself as you worked to heal others and that the jobs you had were ones that you could do around your daughters and from home. I wanted you to shine like the bright star that you are, and I didn't see that you were shining in your own way.

I am happy that you have found love now, something I was unable to do. I want you to know that you deserve that love and that he is lucky to have you, so loyal, loving, kind, generous and devoted to him. I always envied how loving you were with your sister and your dad. I wanted that too. And I wanted to be able to express love like you did.

It was sad, wasn't it. It could have been so much happier.

I don't know if I can shower you with love and admiration. I can thank you for how you helped me in those last years of my life. I didn't deserve your patience and your kindness. I was mean and withholding. I'm sorry you had to ask me to thank you for your help the night before I died, and I appreciate how you stood up for me with your brother when he wanted to move me to LA.

You helped me to die. You told me it was okay to let go and so I did. I needed that help. I would have lingered, and I no longer had a real life. It was time. Just like you told me.

I can see that you were mothering me in ways I did not mother you. You showed up and kept coming even when I was cold and unappreciative. You taught me so much about caring and love with your big heart, your goodness and sweetness, which I always made fun of. I'd taken on the identity of hard and wild and stuck with it even when it no longer served me.

So I'm sorry for all of it. All those thousands, millions of times I didn't express love and appreciation. I want to express it now. I hope it is not too late.

You came along, my fourth child, bright and vibrant, strong and resilient. You couldn't keep up with the older kids but you tried so hard. And you did catch up in many ways.

I was amazed and stunned and sometimes frightened by your determination and power. I threw water on your fire and I'm sorry for that. I could have loved you so much better.

I admire who you are, your resilience, your determination and your power. I am proud that I gave birth to such a strong, intelligent, loving and powerful woman. I can see that you are living your life, searching for the truth of your being, trying to free yourself from unwanted thoughts and baggage. And I now know the value of that work and commend you for your efforts.

In my heart I loved you. I couldn't express it and I'm sorry. I know you felt it that last night before I died, when you stood in the doorway and looked back. Showing you that softness helped me to let go the next day. At least I had given you that. A crumb.

You deserve a feast of love and recognition, no more crumbs. That's over now. Water under the bridge, as I always said. If I could go back and change the story, I would have loved, appreciated and admired you always as the gift to the world that you are.

And thank you for the honor of being your mother. You tried to help me, and I refused. I would welcome it in a different scenario. I would love and cherish you and be able to receive your love back, which would have nourished my own parched heart.

So much misunderstanding. So much pain and wasted time. Too many hours playing solitaire on the computer and drinking gin. I could have been expressing love to you and others, trying to make amends for the harm that I caused. I am so sorry.

I wish you all the love and joy that you so well deserve. I'm asking for your forgiveness. I need that for my own healing.

Life is too short to not love. Love is all. I know that now. The rest does not matter at all. Just love. Express it always, everywhere you can. It matters. I'm so sorry I didn't.

Please accept my love now.

An hour late and a dollar short, I know. But love it is.

Now and always,
Mother

Dear Mom,

Thank you so much for your letter. I appreciate all your apologies and am glad that you now have a clearer and wiser perspective on life and love.

Yes, it was such a sad story and so much pain. And it could have been so light and loving. But that is over now. Now we need to move on and learn from it all.

I want to let in your love and appreciation to heal my own heart. I want to do that. It may take a little time, but I promise to be open to it and to let it in.

I need you to keep sending it my way.

I do forgive you for the pain you carried and how you inflicted it onto me. I learned a lot about the plight of being human from our relationship.

I wish you well in your healing and journey.

Sending you love,
Diane

As you can see from reading these letters, this is a powerful exercise. You get to witness and experience a deep energetic shift that allows a healing to occur on many levels.

I have tried this process myself, as well as with clients, and I am always deeply moved at what transpires. Even though the letters and circumstances are all very different, the theme of forgiveness and love remains the same throughout.

I encourage you to try this in your own life. Is there anyone in your life that you need to forgive? Is there anyone you need closure with? Is there anyone that you need more love and acceptance from? There may be more than one person. I would pick the relationship that feels the heaviest and start with that one.

Now imagine this person just sat down to write you a letter. Grab a pen, take a deep breath and let the writing flow. Don't think, just let the words come. Let this person explain themselves. Let them apologize. Let them say how proud they are of you and let them shower you with the love you always wished they had given you.

Allow them to tell you whatever you feel like you need to hear in order to feel whole again. Let the goodness soak into your skin, your mind, your heart. How does it feel to hear the words you always wanted to hear? How will this positively affect your life? How will you show up differently now?

Now write them back and notice if you have a different perspective. Maybe you have more compassion around why they behaved the way they did. Maybe you finally feel seen, heard, understood and loved. Maybe you are ready to accept their apology and move on.

This is an opportunity to get closure and to heal old wounds, both with people living and with those who have passed away. I'm not suggesting you use this exercise to reestablish relationships with people who have hurt you. This is simply a way to experience a healing with someone who may never apologize or love you in the way that you need to be loved.

You may have to do this exercise several times. You may have to do this exercise with many different people. It all depends on how much healing needs to occur.

In my mom's circumstance, a few years after she had the correspondence with her mother, she felt like there was more to forgive. I had just shared my book idea with her and she was inspired to write a love letter to her Soul.

She sat down to write it and found herself asking her Soul to help her forgive her mother. She knew she was ready to let the pain go, but she also knew she needed Divine help to let it go completely. This is what my mom wrote to me after she wrote the letter to her Soul.

"Dearest Heather,

I got inspired to write a letter to my Soul last night, asking it to help me to forgive my mother. To let it all go. I sat and

wept for the whole time that I wrote to it and it wrote me
back. It felt deep and huge to face that again.
I know that it helped and when I stand in my Soul,
all is forgiven."

Wow. I love that last line. "When I stand in my Soul, all is forgiven." So powerful and true.

This writing exercise can act as a catalyst to open up the locked chains around our hearts and to allow in a miraculous healing that is essential for our greatest evolution and happiness. It can help us to safely navigate our way through the pain to the other side, where a broader perspective and more compassion are waiting for us with open arms.

You can use this exercise in any form. Maybe you are the one who hurt someone and so you write a letter apologizing to them. Maybe you need to forgive yourself for something you did and so you use this exercise to explore what it would take to forgive and let go. What would you need to say? What would you need to hear? Who would you be if you could let this go?

Everyone I know who has tried this exercise, including myself, always reports feeling lighter, freer and happier afterward. It gives us a deeper perspective of all that was going on in our life at that time.

Try this writing exercise in your own life. It is an opportunity to get closure, to forgive and to let go and most importantly, to set yourself free to live your beautiful and precious life.

CHAPTER TEN

Love Letters with Sadness and Fear

I used to deeply resist the presence of sadness and fear in my life. I was more interested in making it go away than uncovering the possible message it may be carrying for me. I felt victimized by it and often powerless to it.

If you are experiencing sadness or fear in your life, it can be very useful to dialogue with it. Maybe you are experiencing grief and sadness from the loss of someone in your life or fear and worry about a future event or you just feel sad and anxious and you aren't sure why. Whatever the case, reach out to your emotions and be curious about what they might reveal to you.

The first time I wrote to sadness and fear, I was experiencing a lot of unexplained sadness and anxiety and I found myself in some kind of dark night of the Soul. Except it wasn't one night. I could have handled one night. It was many nights that turned into days, weeks, and months.

It felt like every buried emotion was knocking on my door to be acknowledged, seen, heard and ultimately set free. It was exhausting and uncomfortable.

I tried to ignore it, numb it, push through it, go around it, avoid it, and run away from it, but the cries of agony only got louder.

So, one day I stopped. I stopped running.

I thought to myself, what if sadness and fear aren't the problem? What if my *resistance* to sadness and fear is the problem?

I had spent so much time and energy avoiding these uninvited emotions. What if I could just be with them and accept them? What if nothing is broken and nothing needs to be numbed out or fixed?

As I sat in this reflection, I knew I had to drop down deeper and face my emotions head on. I wrote my sadness and fear a love letter to try and make amends and to figure it all out, and here is what transpired.

Dear Sadness and Fear,

I resist your presence in my life. I feel uncomfortable and I want to crawl out of my body to escape the pain I feel. I want to numb out so I don't hear your loud, sad, scary song.

I write this letter to make amends. I am sorry for fiercely resisting you in every area of my life. I realize how broken I have felt at times, but I am ready and willing to see things differently.

I have run from you for so long. Please forgive me for making you feel uninvited. What do you need me to understand? I want to love you and accept you exactly as you are, but I don't know how to do that. I feel sad and worthless.

Why do I feel this way? My instinct is to make you go away. I want to learn how to appreciate you and to learn from you. Please help me to know what to do.

I hope I can learn to embrace, accept and love all aspects of myself. To be able to be with it all and stay connected to the deeper truth of who I am. I'm ready to learn, grow, evolve and embody the love and light that is within and all around.

Thank you for helping me to know what to do. I am ready to listen and to receive your helpful wisdom.

Love,
Heather

Dearest Heather,

Wow. Thank you for reaching out. We appreciate your honesty and we accept your apology. Your reflection is spot-on. Thank you for finally accepting us. We are not here to hurt you. You are not broken. There is nothing wrong.

Please trust us when we say that everything is going to be okay. I know this time is uncomfortable. It is supposed to be. Stop running and let yourself feel the pain. It has to be felt and then it will move on. You will not feel like this forever.

Right now, you are in the fire, burning off old stories, old ideas, old sadness. It is all coming up so it can finally be set free. But you cannot run from it. You have to face it. You are strong and can handle this.

Everything is a lesson to take you deeper and ultimately to set you free from the appearance of the roller coaster in your life. You are not the highs and lows, good and bad, broken and fixed. Those are all illusions and ideas based in a right-wrong world.

There is no right and wrong. The emotions feel real but the only realness lies in the stillness, peace and love that you embody on a deeper level.

You are part of the powerful, strong, omnipotent ocean. You are not the waves. Don't spend any more energy resisting. Let the waves rise and fall.

You can handle your life. You can handle your emotions. They don't define you. Emotions are only here to help guide you to a more meaningful way of existing. Relax and use your energy to go deeper and let yourself flow within the magic of your life.

You don't have to figure everything out. You don't have to take it all so seriously. This lifetime is a short blip on the radar of your existence. You existed before this lifetime and you will exist beyond this lifetime. You are already free. True freedom does not lie in the good or bad emotions of your life.

Welcome it all in because it cannot hurt you or define you. Let it all go because it cannot heal you or make you better. You are already whole and complete. This is not a theory. This is the truth. You are already whole and complete. Let that sink in.

Ask yourself empowering questions and marinate in the possibilities. Who are you in the truth of your wholeness? Who are you in the truth of there is nothing to fix? Who are you if nothing is broken? Spend your time analyzing those questions and live from that place.

Feel into the miracles that surround you now and exist beyond space, time and the illusions of this world. You are a part of something much bigger than meets the eye. You can trust in the trillions of stars that are always lighting your path in the Universe.

You are already complete. You are already whole and you are already free my love. You are already free.

We love you and we stand with you in your strength, love and brilliance.

Love,
Sadness and Fear

After I re-read what had transpired, I sat quietly pondering the questions, "Who am I if nothing is broken?" "Who am I in the truth of there is nothing to fix?" "Who am I in the truth of my wholeness?"

My mind was quiet. My sadness had shifted. My fear had subsided. I was looking at my life from a different angle, with a deeper, wider lens. Much like the healing in my body, this initial letter correspondence helped me shift the energy around sadness and fear.

Because I stopped running from it, I was able to be in a new place with it all. It was as if my willingness to turn towards the sadness and to hear what it had to say sent a message to the Universe that I was ready to heal.

Shortly after this correspondence, I found a profoundly helpful therapist who has taught me how to safely explore and understand myself on a deeper level and I have been able to heal, release and transform so many old, stuck emotions.

Now feelings of sadness and fear don't bother me like they used to. When those emotions rise up, I ask empowering questions. I wonder what this is here to teach me? I wonder what I need to release and let go of? I wonder how I can heal and transform from this?

I don't wallow in it or feel victimized by it. I turn towards it. I give it a voice and I let it share its wisdom with me.

So, if you ever find yourself lost in worry, anxiety, sadness or fear, try this simple exercise. Face your emotions in a loving way. Give them a voice. Maybe they are trying to tell you something. Maybe they just need to be acknowledged.

Hear them, see them, and let them say whatever they need to say. Allow yourself to experience your wholeness, where nothing is broken. Invite the darkness into the light and welcome it all in.

CHAPTER ELEVEN

Love Letters with Joy

Joy is a blissful bonus of life and it wants to bubble up in our experiences. I know for myself, I allow joy to flow in for big moments that seem worthy like birthdays and special events but I often overlook all the micro moments that contain macro levels of joy. When I take the time to make space for the joy that wants to be a part of my daily life, I am rewarded with laughter, happiness and bliss.

Writing a love letter to joy is especially important after you have corresponded with your sadness or your fear. An easy way to help yourself rise up and feel better, is to write a love letter to joy or any feeling that brings you joy. For example you could write to laughter, peace or happiness. Invite these qualities and experiences back into your life.

Here is an example of a love letter that I wrote to joy to reconnect and consciously invite it back into my life.

Dearest Joy,

I love you so much. When I feel you in my life, everything feels magical. How can I experience more of you? How can I let you in?

I try to invite you into my life everyday because I tend to crowd you out accidentally. My worries push the joy away. And yet I crave you. I long to feel you and be carefree, joyful and joy-filled.

I want to rejoice in everything that I have and everything that I am. I want to bring joy everywhere I go and to give it away to everyone I meet. I want to laugh and to enjoy everything.

Thank you for making my life fun and for abundantly loving me through it all. I am so grateful for you.

Love,
Heather

Dearest Heather,

What a gift to receive your letter. I love to feel your joyful love. Joy is seeking you just as much as you are seeking it.

Joy is your birthright. You don't have to earn it or prove you are worthy. Joy is the truth of who you are. The worries are clouds, but joy is the sun itself and it is always present, even if you can't see it or feel it.

Keep inviting joy in. It matters that you long for it and look for it. It matters that you crave it and desire to give it away. It is abundantly available for you and everyone always and in all ways. Open your arms to receive joy and enjoy it all.

I joyfully adore everything that you are and I rejoice in your joy-filled heart.

Love,
Joy

The act of reaching out to joy, allowed joy to reach back and wrap its arms around me. I felt joyful energy flowing within and all around me. This simple correspondence created joyful, rejuvenating, peaceful bliss.

Make space for peace and joy again and set the intention to actively search for things that light you up on a daily basis.

Lift yourself up.

Help yourself heal.

Give yourself permission to joyfully thrive.

CHAPTER TWELVE

Love Letters for Releasing Anger

Writing a love letter to release anger may seem like a contradiction, because it doesn't look like a love letter. I still call it a love letter because my deepest intention is to return to love. Writing out my anger has been incredibly therapeutic in my life. Anger was not an emotion that I was comfortable feeling or expressing for many years. However, on my healing journey, I have uncovered unexpressed anger that I had stuffed and suppressed throughout the years and I needed a safe way to express it.

This writing exercise provides a safe space to let it out. I give myself full permission to say anything and everything in these letters. Afterwards, I rip them up into tiny pieces and throw them away. They are not intended for anyone else to see or to read. They are hurtful, raw, mean and ugly. I am often shocked at what pours out. It feels like my pen can't write fast enough.

At first, I thought writing out the anger was bad because I was giving it attention and therefore giving it more power. However, it has had the opposite effect. Turning towards the anger and listening to what it has to say, gives it a chance to be heard and then it is free to leave.

Anger is a powerful emotion and it carries valuable messages for us to see, hear and know. Anger sets boundaries. Anger says, "I'm done. I won't live like this anymore." Anger says, "Don't ever talk to me like that again." Anger says, "What you did was wrong and you need to apologize."

If you have anger towards someone or something, try writing them a letter and give yourself permission to say anything and everything. This is a safe space, so don't hold anything back. You can say things like 'I hate you' or 'I hate it when you act like this' or 'how dare you' or 'you should be ashamed of yourself.' Be mean, be real, be honest.

Then let them write you back and have them apologize to you. Have them explain themselves.   Have them say whatever you need to hear in order to feel better.

After I write a letter like this, I re-read it with the intention to release the emotions. I use EFT Tapping (Emotional Freedom Technique) to tap on acupressure points as I read the words because it helps the emotions leave. You can do a quick google search and find lots of helpful information on EFT and its benefits.

After reading the letter, you could also jump around, yell or hit a pillow. Anything that helps give the energy of the anger a way out of your body. Then it is time to rip up the letter into tiny pieces and throw it away.

This is a very important step. The act of ripping up the letter and throwing it in the trash is energetically getting rid of all the old, angry emotions. You are literally taking out the trash in your mind. Ripping up the letter also ensures that it won't accidentally fall into the wrong hands.

I don't have examples to show you because I don't save these types of letters. But I can say that they have been deeply therapeutic in my life. When I give myself a safe space to be totally honest with my thoughts and emotions, I am relieved at how much better I feel afterward.

I am always surprised at how much emotion comes out onto the paper and I am often stunned at what the person writes back to me. Yes, it is technically me moving the pen, but I somehow channel their voice and personality.

What happens next is even more astonishing. I have had the person I was writing to reach out and apologize to me. Or I am with them and they just seem nicer and easier to be around. Or they act the same, but I don't get triggered by their behavior anymore. The anger has been transformed and everyone involved is set free.

This process can help you move out of anger and back into a place of peace and clarity. Then you can decide if an actual conversation needs to happen with that person. When I take the time to write out my anger in this way, I am less reactive in real life situations and conversations. I am able to respond with clarity and solutions.

Here is something I wrote to help me set a clear intention to release the anger, sadness, dysfunction and old patterns, in order to make room for all the goodness that wants to come into my life. You can read it out loud to empower yourself and set yourself free.

Today I shine a light on all this dysfunction. This is the kind of purge I need to clear away the old and make way for what is possible. I'm willing to let it all come out. I'm giving myself a safe place to express it all.

I hate how ugly it is. It makes me so uncomfortable. I am ashamed to even have these emotions. But I am willing to give all of this fear and anger a voice so I can let it all go and create space for the love to flow in.

Love is so much bigger than this. Love has mercy on all of it. Love is all forgiving. Love can use it all. Love can heal it all. Love can make it all okay.

By turning towards these emotions, I am allowing them all to be seen. They are no longer hidden. They are no longer stuffed feelings.

No wonder I was trying to control everything. I was afraid to be with these emotions. I don't have to be afraid anymore. It's okay to feel them. I have to feel them in order to heal.

This is where the magic happens. This is where radical forgiveness, transformation and new beginnings emerge.

I am giving it all to a loving force stronger than me. I am allowing this loving force to transform all of the old, stagnant energy into light and love. I am allowing myself to be forgiven.

All miracles are held in trust for me and today I am ready to receive them.

Today I am allowing God to set us all free.
Today I am saying sorry and I am open to being forgiven.
Today I am willing to see it all differently.
Today I take my power back.
Today I am open to see it all with fresh eyes, a peaceful mind and a loving heart.
Today I allow myself to open my arms and to welcome in new ways of being, experiencing, living and loving.

I can see clearly now.
My heart is open.
There is peace in my body.
We are all set free.
Thank you, Thank you, Thank you.

Anger is energy and it is here to help you know what you don't like. Be curious about what it is telling you. It is fuel and it can move mountains in your life if you use it in a safe way.

CHAPTER THIRTEEN

Love Letters with a Higher Consciousness

When we connect with love in any form, we are connecting with a higher consciousness. The act of writing a love letter with the intention of receiving help and finding comfort, is a form of prayer. When we keep the pen moving and allow ourselves to be responded to, it can feel like an answer to our prayers.

I love writing love letters with God because it gives me a direct experience of Divine, unconditional love and for that I will be forever grateful. When I allow myself to be loved unconditionally, my body relaxes and heals, my heart opens, my mind becomes peaceful and I am able to give and receive kind, patient, helpful love to myself and others.

I know God is a loaded word for many people, but for me, God means Love. Unconditional, limitless, boundless, healing love. When I align with that love, my life feels miraculous and purposeful. When I forget to align with it, life can feel disjointed and often challenging. My letters are a quick way to realign and reconnect with God and the Divine Loving energy that flows within and all around us.

Sometimes my letters are filled with gratitude and thanks and sometimes they are loaded with fear and worry and I am seeking answers and comfort. When I allow myself to receive help from God and Divine Love, my problems find solutions with Divine ease and grace. I am always comforted with the wisdom and guidance that comes through the higher consciousness and onto the paper.

When I write these letters, I write as if what I am praying for is already here and happening. For example, I write "Thank you for helping me release this pain" instead of "Please help me release this pain." Say it out loud and you will feel the difference. "Please help me" has a pleading energy. I am here and what I want is over there.

"Thank you for helping me" has the energy that what I need and want is already happening and it brings a sense of peace to my mind and body. When we can relax and feel like it is already done, then we are in the right vibration to receive that which we deeply desire.

I have written so many love letters to God and Divine Love over the years, it was hard to pick just one. Each letter carries wisdom and powerful messages of love.

Sometimes I write to just one loving entity and other times I write to several. Use the word or words that feel right for you. It's all love, so there is no right or wrong way to do it.

Here is one of my letters that helped me reconnect and receive Divine loving, healing energy and helpful guidance.

Dearest God and Divine Love,

Thank you for being real and a part of who I am. Thank you for my life and the lives of all the people I love. Thank you for protecting us, guiding us and loving us through it all. Thank you for the awareness of my wholeness and my connection to you. It is peace and comfort beyond my wildest dreams.

Thank you for your clear and loving presence. I am so grateful to see you and feel you everywhere. I feel safe and protected. Through your love, I feel a deep peace that I have longed for my whole life.

This limitless love is the guide, the teacher, the mentor, the supporter, the crystal ball, the kindness and the love that I have been searching for outside of myself. You were with me all along.

The fog has lifted, my vision has been restored. I feel your abundant abundance, peaceful peace, and loving love. It is limitless, endless, boundless and free.

Thank you for always being there for me, even when I refused to let you in. I'm so sorry for all the times I turned my back on love. Thank you for helping me to forgive and to be forgiven.

Thank you for helping me to remain soft, flexible, open and receptive. Thank you for helping me to remember to give everything to you. I am ready to surrender it all. I cannot continue on the path of resistance and rigidity. I need your help with this.

I am ready to be a carrier of love. Let my heart be open. Let my heart be full of love and love only. That is my highest vision. To be a channel for your deep, healing and transformative love.

Let me live in your truth. Let it become my truth. Let me surrender it all to you, trusting the path and the goodness of life and the Universe.

Thank you for everything. Thank you for being gentle with my mind, Soul, body and spirit. Thank you for every road that has led me to this moment.

I devote my life to your limitless love. I love you and I love being loved by you.

Love,
Heather

Dearest Heather,

Thank you for your gorgeous letter. We appreciate your love and gratitude and we are so happy that you see us, hear us and feel our boundless love for you. We have always been here. Always. We have never left you.

We are always available to help you. Reach out, surrender it all, ask for help, ask for signs, ask for healings, ask for abundance.

We are abundantly here for you. Abundantly available to help you. Abundantly present, peaceful and loving.

We are so proud of you. We appreciate your kindness, your love, your willingness to give love, your encouraging words and your compassionate heart. It all matters. It all adds up. It all makes a difference.

Love is your Divine DNA. You are pure love. Let love rule your life.

Let love be everything that you are. Remember to allow it to flow. To allow it to guide you. To allow love to be bigger and stronger than any other idea, concept, thought or perception.

Our vision is your vision. Our heart is your heart. Our love is your love. Let it flow, my love.

Surrender into the wholeness and enoughness of everything that you are. It is all here. The love is here and available to everyone always.

We are so grateful for your presence, your awareness and your receptivity. Allow yourself the time and space to feel your connection to us everywhere. Breathe it in.

Love is available everywhere, always and in all ways.

Every breath is a ticket to your freedom. Every moment is an opportunity to claim your birthright of love and love only. You are free.

Bask in the glorious truth of your wholeness and your oneness with life. We are all pure love and love is our only purpose.

You don't have to carry it all by yourself. We will always be here to encourage you. We will always help you to find the loving truth in it all. We will listen to you deeply. You can tell us anything.

Allow yourself to come home to this love. We are a safe place and space for you. You don't have to hide parts of yourself. We can hear and handle it all. Allow us the honor of loving you through it all.

Thank you for trusting us to be a source of love,
nourishment and peaceful, healing wisdom.

We love you, we will always love you and we will always
love being loved by you!

Love,
God and Divine Love

I am often left speechless after I read the unconditional love and guidance I receive. It is real, it is practical, it is helpful and it lifts me out and above the fog of my worries, my fears and my dysfunction.

The more that I allow myself to receive unconditional love, the more I am able to give it to myself and to the people I love, and that is a gift I will forever be grateful for.

Writing to this loving energy and asking for guidance has upleveled my life. It is a lifeline to love and helpful, healing energy. It is a love transfusion and I know if it is available to me, then it is available to everyone. May it light up your life and help you as much as it continues to help me.

CHAPTER FOURTEEN

Love Letters as Invitations

Love letters are invitations of love and when we align ourselves with love, anything is possible. Creating and living a life we love can be as simple as asking for what we want and being open to see and receive the goodness that surrounds us in every moment.

Ask yourself, what do I want more of in my life? And then write to that thing/experience/emotion and invite it in.

Believe in the fact that the act of writing to it, will call it into existence, because it will. These invitations create portals for new beginnings and new energy to flow to you.

Invite everything you want into your life. Imagine you are throwing the most sensational party and send out personal invitations to your guests of honor. These can be short and sweet. They can write you back or not but make sure that you mentally hear them RSVPing yes to you!

Here are some fun examples.

Dearest Peace,

Please come into my heart and mind. Take up residence and stay forever. Let's be together always. Wrap your arms around me and everyone on this planet. I want to live and breathe in your grace and wisdom.

Love,
Heather

Dearest Heather,

I am here with you and for you always. We are never separate. If you ever feel separate from me, then slow down and breathe. You will find me again. I love you. Sending you peaceful blessings always.

Love,
Peace

Dearest Creativity,

Please come into my life. Show me what you want me to do. I'm ready to bring whatever you want into the world. Together we can make the world a happier place.

Let's raise the abundance and loving vibration in the world together. I am ready to receive your brilliance.

Thank you for everything. I love you!

Love,
Heather

Dearest Heather,

Thank you for your invitation. I am so excited to create with you. I am here and available, so let's do this and have fun!

Love,
Your Creativity

Dearest Body,

Let's heal and be well. Let's experience vibrant health beyond our wildest dreams. Let's laugh and have fun. Let's enjoy this life together.

I love and adore you and I am so grateful for everything you do for me.

Let's reach our highest potential together.

With love and admiration,
Heather

Dearest Heather,

I love you so much! I am all in with you. Here's to our highest potential of peace, health, joy, love and bliss.

Love,
Your loving body

Dearest Abundance,

Thank you for everything I have. I am so blessed. Thank you for continuing to shower me in your goodness.

I have open arms to receive your blissful blessings and I am forever grateful for your presence in my life.

Love,
Heather

Dearest Heather,

Thank you my love. I love being seen and appreciated by you. I am here always and I love showering you with limitless, boundless abundance!

I abundantly love you!

Love,
Abundance

Dearest Laughter,

I love it when you visit me. I am ready to laugh more and to see the humor in myself and in my life. Thank you for coming every day, all throughout my days.

You make life so fun. I love the way you make me feel.

Thank you for everything and everyone who has made me laugh.

Love,
Heather

Dearest Heather,

I love being in your life. Your laugh carries so much joy. Thank you for being open to receive me. I promise to show up more.

With joyful love,
Laughter

Those are just a few examples of how simple this process can be. As you can see, we can write to anything and everything in our lives. It is a way to remind our mind of how we want to live, who we want to be and where we want to focus.

The Universe gives us what we are interested in, so let's get interested in the things that light us up and bring us joy. May this exercise invite in your most extraordinary life possible and shower you with love.

CHAPTER FIFTEEN

A Love Letter to You

Thank you so much for using your precious time to read this book. Thank you for being open to finding new ways to connect with yourself and to set yourself free.

I see your brilliance and I know you contain a guidance system within that will lead you back to your heart and help you create a future you love. I hope this love letter writing process brings more peace and healing into your life.

You hold many keys to unlock your amazing potential, passions and purpose. Reconnecting with yourself through writing will ignite your spirit and your capacity to love and be loved.

Tap into the deep wells of wisdom and love that are within you. The time is now and you have always been ready.

I will end with one final love letter, a love letter to you.

Dearest Reader,

Thank you for being here. I appreciate your willingness and openness. Allow yourself to live in the wonder of your life.

Let yourself explore, engage and participate. Ask questions and be curious.

You don't have to know everything and you don't have to figure it all out. You can't do "it" wrong. There is so much freedom within you and all around you. Feel into the playfulness and the joyfulness that is intertwined in every experience.

Nothing is lost. Nothing is wasted. Nothing is missing.

Bask in the wholeness of who you are. Make time for the part of you that sees, feels, knows and embodies the loving truth of everything.

It is a privilege to be alive right now, so give yourself permission to enjoy it all.

Relax and let your vision and intuitive perspective expand into the miraculous realm that loves your attention and presence. This is where your heart, mind, body, Soul and spirit can thrive.

The time is now and you have always been ready.

Let yourself step wholeheartedly into your birthright of freedom, abundance, love, peace, and joy.

I believe in you and I am grateful for you.

Thank you, thank you, thank you.

Wishing you endless blessings on your journey!

Love,
Heather

Acknowledgements:

Thank you to everyone who helped me write and edit this book. I appreciate your willingness and kindness. You know who you are and I couldn't have finished this book without you.

An extra special thanks to my mom who bought me my first journal, encouraged me to write and whose extraordinary writing talents have inspired me throughout my life.

Thank you to my loving husband who supports me in everything that I do.

Thank you to my children who have opened my heart and have taught me how to love in bigger and more meaningful ways.

Thank you to my spiritual teachers and mentors throughout the years who have lifted me up and guided me home.

Thank you to God, Divine Love and my Soul for showing me unconditional, healing love, and for always returning me back to love.

Thank you to my love letters for helping me, accepting me and loving me through it all.

Thank you to all my friends, family and love itself. You make every moment worth living.

I love you all!